The
Language
of
Friendship

The language of friendship is not
words, but meanings 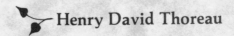 It is an
intelligence above language

—Henry David Thoreau

Other books by

Blue Mountain Arts inc.

Come Into the Mountains, Dear Friend
by Susan Polis Schutz
I Want to Laugh, I Want to Cry
by Susan Polis Schutz
Peace Flows from the Sky
by Susan Polis Schutz
The Best Is Yet to Be
Step to the Music, Vol. I
Step to the Music, Vol. II
The Desiderata of Happiness

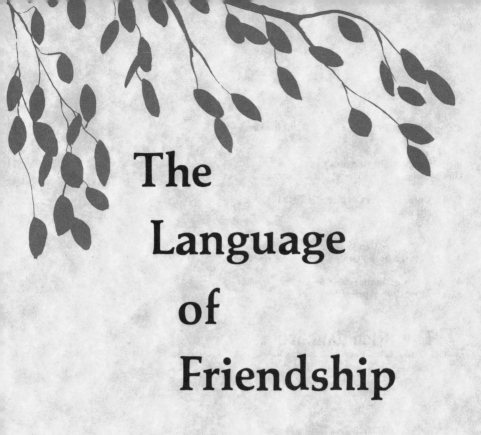

The Language of Friendship

Edited by Susan Polis Schutz

Designed and Illustrated
by Stephen Schutz

Blue
Mountain
Arts inc.
Boulder, Colorado

Library of Congress Catalog: 74-29431
ISBN Number: 0-88396-010-9

Layout by Roger Ben Wilson
Manufactured in the United States of America

First Printing: January, 1975
Second Printing: April, 1975

Blue Mountain Arts inc.
P.O. Box 4549 Boulder, Colorado 80302

ACKNOWLEDGMENTS

The following poems by Susan Polis Schutz have appeared earlier; *Man is forced to be alone* and *You know how I feel,* © copyright 1972 by Continental Publications; *Someone,* © copyright 1973 by Continental Publications; *I haven't seen you,* and *There is no need,* © copyright 1974 by Continental Publications.

We gratefully acknowledge the permission granted by the following authors, publishers, and authors' representatives to reprint poems from their publications. Recognition is also made to poets and original publishers for the use of many poems which are now in the public domain.

Harcourt, Brace, Jovanovich, Inc. for *I am so glad and very,* from *Complete Poems 1913-1962* by E. E. Cummings, © copyright 1940 by E. E. Cummings, copyright 1968 by Marion Morehouse Cummings. Reprinted by permission of Harcourt, Brace, Jovanovich, Inc.

A careful effort has been made to trace the ownership of poems used in this anthology in order to get permission to reprint copyright poems and to give proper credit to the copyright owners.

If any error or omission has occurred, it is completely inadvertent, and we would like to correct it in future editions provided that written notification is made to the publisher, BLUE MOUNTAIN ARTS, INC., P.O. Box 4549, Boulder, Colorado 80302.

CONTENTS

WHAT IS A FRIEND?

What is a friend? I will tell you ❦
It is a person with whom you dare
to be yourself ❦ Your soul can be naked
with him ❦ He seems to ask of you
to put on nothing, only to be what you
are ❦ He does not want you to be
better or worse ❦ When you are with
him, you feel as a prisoner feels
who has been declared innocent ❦ You
do not have to be on your guard.
You can say what you think, so long as it
is genuinely you ❦ He understands
those contradictions in your nature that
lead others to misjudge you ❦
With him you breathe freely ❦ You can
avow your little vanities and envies
and hates and vicious sparks, your mean-
nesses and absurdities and, in opening
them up to him, they are lost, dissolved on
the white ocean of his loyalty ❦

He understands ᴑ You do not have to be
careful ᴑ You can abuse him,
neglect him, tolerate him ᴑ Best of all,
you can keep still with him ᴑ It
makes no matter ᴑ He likes you—he is
like fire that purges to the bone ᴑ
He understands ᴑ He understands ᴑ
You can weep with him, sin with him,
laugh with him, pray with him ᴑ
Through it all—and underneath—he sees,
knows and loves you ᴑ A friend?
What is a friend? Just one, I repeat,
with whom you dare to be yourself ᴑ ᴑ

C. Raymond Beran

Don't walk in front of me
   I may not follow
Don't walk behind me
   I may not lead
Walk beside me
And just be my friend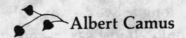

— Albert Camus

All men have their frailties,
and whoever looks for a friend without
imperfections will never find what
he seeks.

So long as we love, we serve.
So long as we are loved by others, I
would almost say we are indispensable;
and no man is useless while he
has a friend.

We are all travellers in the wilderness
of this world, and the best that we find
in our travels is an honest friend.

Robert Louis Stevenson

The only way to have a friend
is to be one.

A friend may well be reckoned the
masterpiece of nature.

A friend is a person with whom I may be
sincere. Before him, I may think aloud.

The glory of friendship is not
the outstretched hand, nor the kindly
smile nor the joy of companionship; it is
the spirited inspiration that comes
to one when he discovers that someone
else believes in him and is willing
to trust him.

Ralph Waldo Emerson

O friend, my bosom said,
Through thee alone the sky is arched,
Through thee the rose is red,
All things through thee take nobler form,
And look beyond the earth,
The mill-round of our fate appears
A sun-path in thy worth.
Me, too, thy nobleness has taught
To master my despair;
The fountains of my hidden life
Are through thy friendship fair.

A true friend is somebody who can make us do what we can. 🍃

God evidently does not intend us all to be rich, or powerful, or great, but He does intend us all to be friends. 🍃🍃

Ralph Waldo Emerson

I SAW IN LOUISIANA A LIVE-OAK GROWING

I saw in Louisiana a live-oak growing,
All alone stood it and the moss hung down from
    the branches,
Without any companion it grew there uttering joyous
    leaves of dark green,
And its look, rude, unbending, lusty, made me think
    of myself,
But I wonder'd how it could utter joyous leaves
    standing alone there without its friend near, for I
    knew I could not,
And I broke off a twig with a certain number of leaves
    upon it, and twined around it a little moss,
And brought it away, and I have placed it in sight
    in my room,
It is not needed to remind me as of my own
    dear friends,
(For I believe lately I think of little else than of them,)
Yet it remains to me a curious token, it makes me think
    of manly love;
For all that, and though the live-oak glistens there
    in Louisiana solitary in a wide flat space,
Uttering joyous leaves all its life without a friend
    a lover near,
I know very well I could not.

I have learned that to be with those
I like is enough.

I hear it was charged against me that I sought to
   destroy institutions,
But really I am neither for nor against institutions,
Only I will establish in Manahatta and in every city
   of these States, inland and seaboard,
And in the fields and woods, and above every keel
   little or large that dents the water,
The institution of the dear love of comrades.

Walt Whitman

There are plenty of acquaintances
in the world, but very few real friends.

Chinese Proverb

You can hardly make a friend in a year,
but you can lose one in an hour.

Chinese Proverb

Have no friends not equal to yourself.

There are three friendships which
are advantageous, and three which are
injurious. Friendship with the upright;
friendship with the sincere; and
friendship with the man of much observa-
tion; these are advantageous.
Friendship with the man of specious airs;
friendship with the insinuatingly soft;
and friendship with the glib-tongued;
these are injurious.

                                    Confucius

Though I am different from you,
We were born involved in one another.

                                    Tau Ch'ien

A faithful friend is a sturdy shelter
He that has found one
Has found a treasure

Ecclesiasticus 6:14

Love Thy Neighbor as Thyself

Leviticus 19:18

חָבֵד נֶאֱמָן

A friendless man is like a left hand without a right.

Hebrew Proverb

Two are better than one; because they have a good reward for their labor. For if they fall, the one will lift up his fellow; but woe to him that is alone when he falleth; for he hath not another to help him up. And if one prevail against him, two shall withstand him; and a threefold cord is not quickly broken.

Old Testament

صَدَاقَة

A friend is one
to whom one may pour
out all the contents
of one's heart,
chaff and grain together
knowing that the
gentlest of hands
will take and sift it,
keep what is worth keeping
and with a breath of kindness
blow the rest away

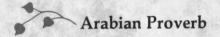 Arabian Proverb

Friendship is, strictly speaking,
reciprocal benevolence, which inclines
each party to be solicitous for the
welfare of the other as for his own.
This equality of affection is created and
preserved by a similarity of disposition
and manners ⧉⧉

True friendship between two people
is infinite and immortal ⧉⧉

Plato

⧉⧉⧉⧉⧉⊠⧉⧉⧉⧉⧉

He who throws away a friend is as bad
as he who throws away his life ⧉⧉

Sophocles

Instead of herds of oxen, endeavor
to assemble flocks of friends about
your house ❧ ❧

Epictetus

One of the most beautiful qualities
of true friendship is to understand and
to be understood ❧ ❧

Seneca

If a man could mount to Heaven
and survey the mighty universe, his
admiration of its beauties would
be much diminished unless he had a friend
to share in his pleasure

Friendship renders prosperity
more brilliant, while it lightens adversity
by sharing it and making its burden
common

Never injure a friend, even in jest

Cicero

A MILE WITH ME

O who will walk a mile with me
  Along life's merry way?
A comrade blithe and full of glee,
Who dares to laugh out loud and free,
And let his frolic fancy play,
Like a happy child, through the flowers gay
That fill the field and fringe the way
  Where he walks a mile with me.

And who will walk a mile with me
  Along life's weary way?
A friend whose heart has eyes to see
The stars shine out o'er the darkening lea,
And the quiet rest at the end o' the day,—
A friend who knows, and dares to say,
The brave, sweet words that cheer the way
  Where he walks a mile with me.

With such a comrade, such a friend,
I fain would walk till journeys end,
Through summer sunshine, winter rain,
And then?—Farewell, we shall meet again!

But, after all, the very best thing
in good talk, and the thing that helps
most, is friendship. How it dissolves
the barriers that divide us, and
loosens all constraint, and diffuses itself
like some fine old cordial through
all the veins of life—this feeling that we
understand and trust each other, and
wish each other heartily well! Everything
into which it really comes is good.

Henry Van Dyke

A HOME SONG

I read within a poet's book
  A word that starred the page:
"Stone walls do not a prison make,
  Nor iron bars a cage!"

Yes, that is true, and something more:
  You'll find, where'er you roam,
That marble floors and gilded walls
  Can never make a home.

But every house where Love abides,
  And Friendship is a guest,
Is surely home, and home-sweet-home:
  For there the heart can rest

These are the things I prize
  And hold of dearest worth;
Light of the sapphire skies,
Peace of the silent hills,
Shelter of the forests,
  comfort of the grass,
Music of birds, murmur of little rills,
Shadows of clouds that swiftly pass,
  And, after showers,
  The smell of flowers,
And of the good brown earth—
And best of all, along the way
    friendship
        and mirth

Henry Van Dyke

The world is so empty if one thinks only of mountains, rivers, and cities; but to know someone who thinks and feels with us, and who, though distant is close to us in spirit, this makes the earth for us an inhabited garden.

—Goethe

It is chance that makes brothers
but hearts that make friends

Von Geibel

The better part of one's life
consists of his friendships

 Abraham Lincoln

A slender acquaintance with the world
must convince every man that actions,
not words, are the true criterion of
the attachment of friends; and that the
most liberal profession of good-will
is very far from being the surest mark of it

 George Washington

i am so glad and very
merely my fourth will cure
the laziest self of weary
the hugest sea of shore

so far your nearness reaches
a lucky fifth of you
turns people into eachs
and cowards into grow

our can'ts were born to happen
our mosts have died in more
our twentieth will open
wide a wide open door

we are so both and oneful
night cannot be so sky
sky cannot be so sunful
i am through you so i

—e. e. cummings

THE ARROW AND THE SONG

I shot an arrow into the air,
It fell to earth, I knew not where;
For, so swiftly it flew, the sight
Could not follow it in its flight.

I breathed a song into the air,
It fell to earth, I knew not where;
For who has sight so keen and strong,
That it can follow the flight of song?

Long, long afterward, in an oak
I found the arrow, still unbroke;
And the song, from beginning to end,
I found again in the heart of a friend.

Let us be what we are and speak
what we think and in all things keep
ourselves loyal to truth and the
sacred professions of friendship

Henry Wadsworth Longfellow

B lessed are they who have the gift
of making friends, for it is one of God's
best gifts ▲ It involves many things,
but above all, the power of going out of
one's self, and appreciating whatever
is noble and loving in another ▲ ▲

If you have a friend worth loving,
Love him, yes, and let him know
That you love him ere life's evening
Tinge his brow with sunset glow;
Why should good words ne'er be said
Of a friend till he is dead?

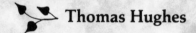 **Thomas Hughes**

THERE IS NO FRIEND
LIKE AN OLD FRIEND

There is no friend like an old friend
Who has shared our morning days.
No greeting like his welcome,
No homage like his praise

Oliver Wendell Holmes

NEW FRIENDS AND OLD FRIENDS

Make new friends, but keep the old;
Those are silver, these are gold.
New-made friendships, like new wine,
Age will mellow and refine.
Friendships that have stood the test
Time and change—are surely best;
Brow may wrinkle, hair grow gray;
Friendship never knows decay.
For 'mid old friends, tried and true,
Once more we reach and youth renew
But old friends, alas! may die;
New friends must their place supply
Cherish friendships in your breast
New is good, but old is best;
Make new friends, but keep the old;
Those are silver, these are gold.

Joseph Parry

This above all: to thine own self be true,
And it must follow, as the night the day,
Thou canst not then be false to any man.

I am not of that feather to shake off
my friend when he must need me.

ALL LOSSES RESTORED

When to the sessions of sweet silent thought
I summon up remembrance of things past,
I sigh the lack of many a thing I sought,
And with old woes new wail my dear time's waste:
Then can I drown an eye, unused to flow,
For precious friends hid in death's dateless night,
And weep afresh love's long since cancell'd woe,
And moan the expense of many a vanish'd sight:
Then can I grieve at grievances foregone,
And heavily from woe to woe tell o'er
The sad account of fore-bemoaned moan,
Which I new pay as if not paid before.
But if the while I think on thee, dear friend,
All losses are restored and sorrows end

William Shakespeare

TAKE TIME

Take time for friendship when you can.
The hours fly swiftly, and the need
That presses on your fellowman
May fade away at equal speed
And you may sigh before the end
That you have failed to play the friend.

Not all life's pride is born of fame;
Not all the joy from work is won.
Too late we hang our heads in shame,
Remembering good we could have done;
Too late we wish that we had stayed
To comfort those who called for aid.

Take time to do the little things
Which leave the satisfactory thought,
When other joys have taken wings,
That we have labored as we ought;
That in a world where all contend,
We often stopped to be a friend.

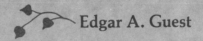 Edgar A. Guest

Friendship is the allay of our sorrows, the ease of our passions, the discharge of our oppressions, the sanctuary to our calamities, the counsellor of our thoughts, the exercise and improvement of what we meditate. ◂ ◂

I account it one of the greatest demonstrations of real friendship, that a friend can really endeavor to have his friend advanced in honor, in reputation, in the opinion of wit or learning, before himself. ◂ ◂

The more we love, the better
we are; and the greater our friendships
are, the dearer we are to God.

By friendship you mean the greatest
love, the greatest usefulness, the
most open communication, the noblest
sufferings, the severest truth, the
heartiest counsel, and the greatest union
of minds of which brave men and
women are capable.

Jeremy Taylor

Someone—
to talk with
to dance with
to sing with
to eat with
to laugh with
to cry with
to think with
to understand
Someone—
to be my friend

You know how I feel
You listen to how I think
You understand . . .
         You're
              my
                   friend

There is no need for an outpouring
of words to explain oneself to a friend.
Friends understand each other's thoughts
even before they are spoken

Susan Polis Schutz

Man is forced to be alone by the
very nature of society. But if you
meet a person who is not envious, who
loves and believes in other than himself,
then to this rare person offer a
lifetime of friendship.

I haven't seen you in a while
yet I often imagine
all your expressions

I haven't spoken to you recently
but many times
I hear your thoughts

Good friends must not always be together
It is the feeling of oneness when distant
that proves a lasting friendship

Susan Polis Schutz

I LOVE YOU

I love you,
Not only for what you are
But for what I am
When I am with you.

I love you
Not only for what
You have made of yourself
But for what
You are making of me.

I love you
for the part of me
That you bring out;
I love you
For putting your hand
Into my heaped-up heart
And passing over
All the foolish, weak things
That you can't help
Dimly seeing there,
And for drawing out
Into the light
All the beautiful belongings
That no one else had looked
Quite far enough to find.

I love you because you

Are helping me to make
Of the lumber of my life
Not a tavern
But a temple;
Out of works
Of my every day
Not a reproach
But a song.

I love you
Because you have done
More than any creed
Could have done
To make me good,
And more than any fate
Could have done
To make me happy.

You have done it
Without a touch,
Without a word,
Without a sign.

You have done it
By being yourself.
Perhaps that is what
Being a friend means,
After all.

Roy Croft

What do we live for, if it is not to make life less difficult to others.

Friendship is the inexpressible comfort of feeling safe with a person having neither to weigh thoughts nor measure words.

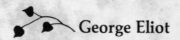 George Eliot

If I can stop one heart from breaking,
I shall not live in vain;
If I can ease one life the aching,
Or cool one pain,
Or help one fainting robin
Unto his nest again,
I shall not live in vain.

Emily Dickinson

If we build on a sure foundation
in friendship, we must love our friends
for their sakes rather than for our own.

Charlotte Bronte

I looked for my soul
but my soul I could not see.
I looked for my God
but my God eluded me.
I looked for a friend
and then I found all three

— Thomas Blake

What made us friends in the long ago
When first we met?
Well, I think I know;
The best in me and the best in you
Hailed each other because they knew
That always and always since life began
Our being friends was part of God's plan

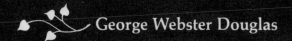 George Webster Douglas

Be true to your word, your work,
and your friend

As I love nature, as I love singing
birds, and gleaming stubble, and flowing
rivers, and morning and evening,
and summer and winter, I love thee
my friend

We do not wish for friends to feed
and clothe our bodies—neighbors are
kind enough for that—but to do the like
office for our spirits

The most I can do for my friend
is simply to be his friend

Think of the importance of friendship in the education of men. It will make a man honest; it will make him a hero; it will make him a saint. It is the state of the just dealing with the just, the magnanimous with the magnanimous, the sincere with the sincere, man with man.

The language of friendship is not words, but meanings. It is an intelligence above language.

Henry David Thoreau